by Michael Dahl

illustrated by Maira Cleste

PICTURE WINDOW BOOKS
a capstone imprint

2

Verbs love action.

Every sentence has a verb.

Many verbs show a physical action, something you can see.

9

Some verbs describe states of being, things you can't see.

10

11

State-of-being verbs are called linking verbs.
They join, or link, a subject to a word (or words)
that names or describes it.

This **is** Sandy Island Beach.

It **seems** very nice.

The sand **feels** amazing between my toes.

Ugh. I **feel** hot and tired.

CRY

FROWN

BREAK

SCARE

TIP

15

16

Some verbs are called helping verbs.

Helping verbs are small words that lend a hand to verbs.

Helping verbs **make** everything a little clearer.

They **HAVE** **helped** us a lot today.

They **WERE** **acting** like real friends.

They **CAN** **share** our snacks.

Those helping verbs are way too cheerful.

I wonder if they scamper.

Despite the crash, I **HAVE BEEN** **enjoying** the day.

Verbs go everywhere.

DRIVE

ROLL

CRUISE

RACE

HONK

CRAWL

Verbs can change to show when something happened or *will* happen. That's called the verb's tense.

"Tense" is like **telling** the time.

Today **is** the present. Yesterday **is** the past. And tomorrow **is** the future.

My pet octopus **bites**. [present tense]

Will it **bite** me? [future tense]

It **bit** my sister yesterday. [past tense]

Today we scamper! Yesterday we scampered!

And tomorrow we will scamper again! Hooray!

The three main verb tenses are present, past, and future.

OUR VERY VALUABLE VERBS

Every sentence has a verb.

I GIVE my dog a hug.
Simon OPENED the book.
The truck tires SQUEAL.
[You] LISTEN!

Verbs are words that show action or states of being. Action verbs describe things that can be seen. State-of-being (or linking) verbs describe things that cannot be seen. They link a subject to a word (or words) that names or describes it.

Archie RACES to the finish line. (action)
The crowd CHEERS. (action)
I AM so happy for him! (state of being)
He IS hot, so he DRINKS some water. (state of being; action)

Helping verbs add information to verbs and make sentences clearer. Forms of "be," "do," and "have" are common helping verbs.

Margo _is_ EATING her lunch.
They _do_ not LIKE peas.
_Do_ you WANT some ice cream?
He _has_ ASKED for pudding.

The tense of a verb tells when something happened. There are three main verb tenses: past, present, future.

The whale SINGS. (present tense; is happening now)
The whale SANG. (past tense; happened in the past)
The whale WILL SING. (future tense; will happen sometime in the future)

ABOUT THE AUTHOR

Michael Dahl is the author of more than 200 books for children and has won the AEP Distinguished Achievement Award three times for his nonfiction. He is the author of the bestselling *Bedtime for Batman* and *You're a Star, Wonder Woman!* picture books. He has written dozens of books of jokes, riddles, and puns. He likes to play with words. In grade school, he read the dictionary for fun. Really. Michael is proud to say that he has always been a noun. A PROPER noun, at that.

ABOUT THE ILLUSTRATOR

Maira Chiodi's colorful, joyful work has appeared in magazines, books, games, and a variety of other products. As a child in Brazil, Maira spent hours cutting paper, painting, and reading—creating wildly imaginative worlds all her own. Today she feels lucky to be able to create and share her illustrations and designs with kids and grown-ups around the world. She divides her time between Canada and Brazil, finding inspiration for her art in nature, animation, and the culture of her native country.

GLOSSARY

action—the act of doing something

helping verb—a word that adds information to a verb about when or if something has a chance of happening

link—to join together

linking verb—a word that joins a subject to a word (or words) that names or describes it; also called a state-of-being verb

physical—having to do with something that can be seen and touched

state of being—how something is, was, or will be

tense—the form a verb takes to show the time it happened; the three main tenses are past, present, and future

verb—a word that shows an action or state of being

THINK ABOUT IT

1. Is the word "kick" an action verb or a state-of-being verb? How about "float" and "is"? Explain your answers.

2. Name the verb tense of the word "ate" in this sentence: **I ate a cookie last night.** Why did you choose that verb tense?

READ MORE

Ayers, Linda. *Kick! Jump! Throw! Run!: Verbs Are Action Words!* Read, Sing, Learn: Songs About the Parts of Speech. Minneapolis: Cantata Learning, 2016.

Fandel, Jennifer. *What Is a Verb?* Parts of Speech. North Mankato, MN: Capstone Press, 2013.

Heinrichs, Ann, and Danielle Jacklin. *Verbs.* Language Rules. New York: AV2 by Weigl, 2018.

INTERNET SITES

Enchanted Learning: Grammar: Verbs
https://www.enchantedlearning.com/grammar/partsofspeech/verbs/index.shtml

Grammaropolis: The Verbs
https://www.grammaropolis.com/verb.php

Schoolhouse Rock: Verbs
https://www.youtube.com/watch?v=US8mGU1MzYw

LOOK FOR ALL THE PARTS OF SPEECH TITLES

31

INDEX

Editor: Jill Kalz
Designer: Lori Bye
Production Specialist: Katy LaVigne
The illustrations in this book were created digitally.

Picture Window Books are published by Capstone
1710 Roe Crest Drive, North Mankato, Minnesota 56003
www.capstonepub.com

Library of Congress Cataloging-in-Publication Data is available on the Library of Congress website.
ISBN 978-1-5158-3870-8 (library binding)
ISBN 978-1-5158-4059-6 (paperback)
ISBN 978-1-5158-3875-3 (eBook PDF)

Summary: Jump! Climb! Lift! Leap! Not known for sitting still, the verbs are packing lots of grammar facts and fun into their parts-of-speech adventure. These quirky, illustrated characters camp, exercise, sail, and swim, and all readers need to do is read, learn, and enjoy!

All internet sites appearing in back matter were available and accurate when this book was sent to press.

Printed and bound in China.
001654